GETTING STARTED

DUPLICATING STENCILS

Stencil plastic (Mylar) can be used; or card wiped over with linseed oil, which left to dry will harden and make the surface waterproof. Place the cut-out stencil on top. Trace around carefully with a permanent pen inside the cut-out shapes. Cut along the lines with a scalpel and remove the pieces. You may prefer to trace on top of the design, then transfer your tracing onto card.

MAKING A SPONGE APPLICATOR

Sponging your stencil is one of the easiest methods, but you may prefer to use a stencil brush, especially for fine detail. Using a piece of upholstery foam or very dense bath sponge, cut pieces 12–50 mm (1/2–2 in) wide and approximately 50 mm (2 in) long. Hold the four corners together and secure with tape to form a pad. You can also round off the ends with scissors or a scalpel and trim to a smooth finish. The small-ended applicators can be used for tiny, intricate patterns.

HOW TO USE WATER-BASED PAINT

Water-based paints are easy and economical to use and have the advantage of drying quickly. For professional-looking stencils, do not load your sponge or brush too heavily or you will not achieve a soft, shaded finish. Paint that is too watery will seep under the stencil edges and smudge. If the paint is too heavy you will obtain a heavy block effect rather than the soft stippling you require.

LOOKING AFTER STENCILS

Stencils have a long life if cared for correctly. Before cleaning make sure you remove any tape or tracing paper that has been added. Remove any excess paint before it dries, and wipe the stencil with a damp cloth every time you use it. If water or acrylic paint has dried and hardened, soften it with water and ease it off gently with a scalpel. Then use a small amount of methylated spirits on a cloth to remove the rest. An oil-based paint can simply be removed by wiping over the stencil with white spirit on a cloth. Stencils should be dried thoroughly before storing flat between sheets of greaseproof paper.

HOW TO USE OIL STICKS

Oil sticks may seem expensive, but in fact go a long way. They take longer to dry, allowing you to blend colours very effectively. Oil sticks are applied with a stencil brush and you need to have a different brush for each colour. Break the seal as instructed on the stick and rub a patch of the colour onto a palette, allowing space to blend colours. As the stencil sticks dry slowly, you need to lift the stencil off cleanly, and replace to continue the pattern.

PRACTISING PAINTING STENCILS

Roll out some lining paper onto a table and select the stencil you wish to practise with. Using spray adhesive, lightly spray the back of your stencil and place it into position on the paper. Prepare your paint on a palette. Dab your sponge or brush into the paint and offload excess paint onto scrap paper. Apply colour over the stencil in a light coat to create an even stippled effect. You can always stencil on a little more paint if a stronger effect is needed, but if you over apply it in the first place it is very difficult to remove. Keep separate sponges for different colours.

PLANNING YOUR DESIGN

Before starting to stencil take time to plan your design. Decide where you want to use the patterns, then work out how to position the stencils so that the design will fit around obstacles such as doorways and corners. The techniques shown here will help you to undertake the job with a systematic approach.

PUTTING PATTERN PIECES TOGETHER

1 Before you apply your design, stencil a sample onto lining paper. Mark the centre and baseline of the design on the paper and put together your pattern pieces. You can then work out the size of the design, how it will fit into the space available and the distance required between repeats.

2 You can avoid stencilling around a corner by working out the number of pattern repeats needed, and allowing extra space either between repeats or within the pattern. Creating vertical lines through the pattern will allow you to stretch it evenly.

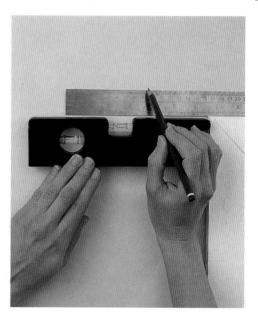

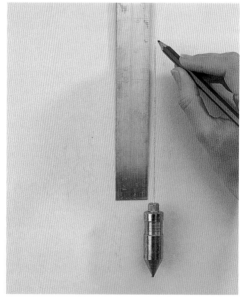

MARKING BASELINES AND HORIZONTAL LINES

Select your stencil area, and take a measure from the ceiling, doorframe, window or edging, bearing in mind the depth of your stencil. Using a spirit level, mark out a horizontal line. You can then extend this by using a chalkline or long ruler with chalk or soft pencil.

MARKING VERTICAL LINES

If you need to work out the vertical position for a stencil, hang a plumbline above the stencilling area and use a ruler to draw a vertical line with chalk or a soft pencil. You will need to use this method when creating an all-over wallpaper design.

FIXING THE STENCIL INTO PLACE

Lightly spray the back of the stencil with spray adhesive, then put it in position and smooth it down carefully. You can use low-tack masking tape if you prefer, but take care not to damage the surface to be stencilled; keep the whole stencil flat to prevent paint seeping underneath.

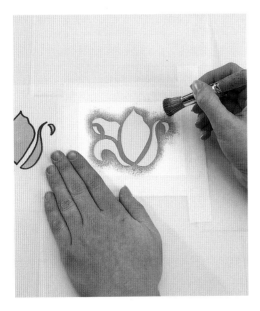

MARKING THE STENCIL FOR A PATTERN REPEAT

Attach a border of tracing paper to each edge of the stencil. Position the next pattern and overlap the tracing paper onto the previous design, tracing over the edge of it. By matching the tracing with the previous pattern as you work along you will be able to align and repeat the stencil at the same intervals.

COPING WITH CORNERS

Stencil around corners after you have finished the rest of the design, having measured to leave the correct space for the corner pattern before you do so. Then bend the stencil into the corner and mask off one side of it. Stencil the open side and allow the paint to dry, then mask off this half and stencil the other part to complete the design.

MASKING OFF PART OF A STENCIL

Use low-tack masking tape to mask out small or intricate areas of stencil. You can also use ordinary masking tape, but remove excess stickiness first by peeling it on and off your skin or a cloth once or twice. To block off inside shapes and large areas, cut out pieces of tracing paper to the appropriate size and fix them on top with spray adhesive.

MITRING STENCIL PATTERNS

1 When you are stencilling a continuous pattern and need to make a corner, mask off the stencil by marking a 45-degree angle at both ends of the stencil with a permanent pen. Mask along this line with a piece of masking tape or tracing paper.

2 Make sure the baselines of the stencil on both sides of the corner are the same distance from the edge, and that they cross at the corner. Put the diagonal end of the stencil right into the corner and apply the paint. Turn the stencil sideways to align the other diagonal end of the stencil and turn the corner.

PAINT EFFECTS

CHOOSING COLOURS

Take care to choose appropriate colours to create the effect you want. Stencil a practice piece onto paper and try a variation of colours to ensure you are pleased with the result. Different colours can make a design look entirely different. Use spray adhesive to fix your practice paper onto the surface on which you wish to produce the design so that you can assess its effect before applying the stencil.

APPLYING WATER-BASED COLOURS

Water-based paint dries quickly, so it tends to layer rather than blend. It is best applied by using a swirling movement or gently dabbing, depending on the finished effect you wish to create. Once you have applied a light base colour, you can add a darker edge for shading. Alternatively, leave some of the stencil bare and add a different tone to that area to obtain a shaded or highlighted appearance.

BLENDING OIL-STICK COLOURS

Oil sticks mix together smoothly and are perfect for blending colours. Place the colours separately on your palette and mix them with white to obtain a variety of tones or blend them together to create new colours. You can also blend by applying one coat into another with a stippling motion while stencilling. Blending looks most effective when applying a pale base coat, then shading on top with a darker colour.

HIGHLIGHTING

A simple way to add highlighting to your design is first to paint in your stencil in a light tone of your main colour, then carefully lift the stencil and move it down a fraction. Then stencil in a darker shade; this leaves the highlighted areas around the top edges of the pattern.

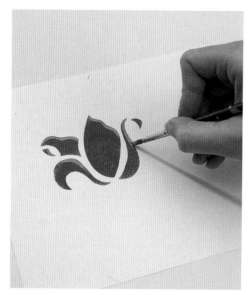

GILDING

After painting your stencil use gold to highlight the edges. Load a fine art brush with gold acrylic paint and carefully outline the top edges of the pattern. Use one quick brush stroke for each pattern repeat, keeping in the same direction. Other methods are to blow bronze powder onto the wet paint, draw around the pattern with a gold flow pen, or smudge on gilt wax cream, then buff to a high sheen.

APPLYING SPRAY PAINTS

Spray paints are ideal on glass, wood, metal, plastic and ceramic surfaces. They are quick to apply and fast drying, but cannot be blended, although you can achieve subtle shaded effects. Apply the paint in several thin coats. Mask off a large area around the design to protect it from the spray, which tends to drift. Try to use sprays out of doors or in a well-ventilated area. Some spray paints are non-toxic, making them ideal for children's furniture.

THE STENCIL COLLECTION
Farmhouse Kitchen
Katrina Hall

Patchwork Tablecloth   8

Carrots & Radishes   12

Peas & Beans   20

Tulips & Chicken Wire   24

Ducks & Chickens Lattice   16

Herbs & Ribbon   28

INTRODUCING STENCILLING

Once you begin stencilling you will be amazed at the wonderful results you can obtain quite easily and without spending a great deal of money. This book introduces six themed projects and provides ready-to-use stencils that can be used with numerous variations in design – just follow the step-by-step features and simple instructions. With very little paint and only a few pieces of equipment you can achieve stunning results. Have fun!

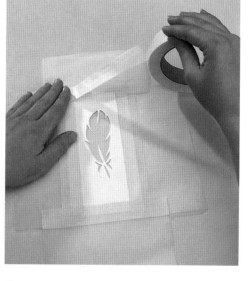

BASIC MATERIALS

Paints and Decorative Finishes
Emulsion paint
Water-based stencil paint
Oil sticks
Acrylic paints (bottles and tubes)
Specialist paints (for fabrics, ceramics, glass etc)
Spray paints
Metallic acrylic artists' colours (gold, silver etc)
Silver and gold art flow pens
Bronze powders (various metallics)
Gilt wax

Brushes and Applicators
Art brushes (variety of sizes)
Stencil brushes (small, medium and large)
Sponge applicators
Mini-roller and tray

Other Equipment
Set square
Blotting paper
Scissors or scalpel (or craft knife)
Roll of lining paper (for practising)
Eraser
Soft pencil
Fine-tip permanent pen
Chalk or Chalkline and powdered chalk
Long rigid ruler
Tape measure
Plumbline
Spirit level
Low-tack masking tape
Spray adhesive
Tracing paper
Paint dishes or palettes
Cloths
Kitchen roll
White spirit
Stencil plastic or card
Cotton buds
Methylated spirits

CUTTING OUT STENCILS
The stencils at the back of the book are all designed to be used separately or together to create many different pattern combinations. Cut along the dotted lines of the individual stencils and make sure you transfer the reference code onto each one with a permanent pen. Carefully remove the cut-out pieces of the stencil. Apply 50 mm (2 in) strips of tracing paper around the edges using masking tape; this will help to prevent smudging paint onto your surface.

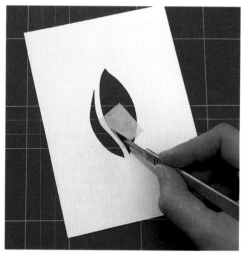

REPAIRING STENCILS
Stencils may become damaged and torn from mishandling, or if the cutouts have not been removed carefully, but they are easy to repair. Keeping the stencil perfectly flat, cover both sides of the tear with masking tape. Then carefully remove any excess tape with a scalpel.

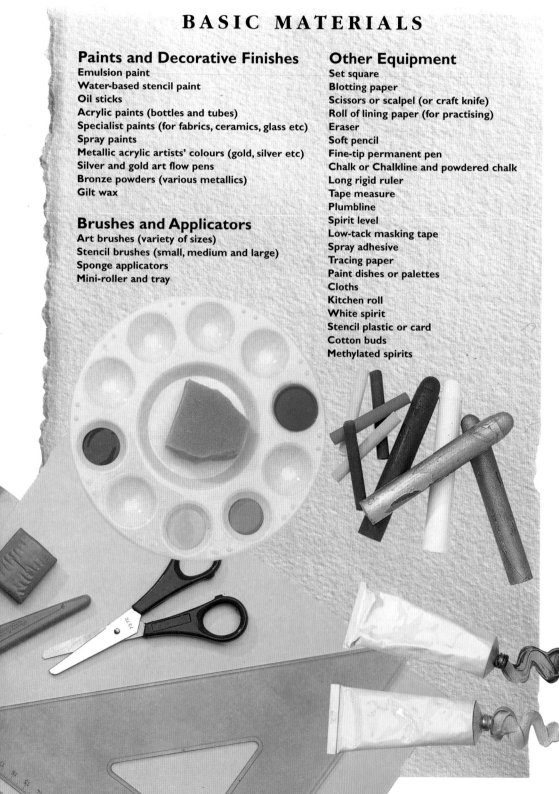

DIFFERENT SURFACES

BARE WOOD

Rub the wood surface down to a smooth finish. Then fix the stencil in place and paint with a thin base coat of white, so that the stencil colours will stand out well when applied. Leave the stencil in place and allow to dry thoroughly, then apply your stencil colours in the normal way. When completely dry you can apply a coat of light wax or varnish to protect your stencil.

PAINTED WOOD

If you are painting wood or medium-density fibreboard (MDF) prior to stencilling, seal it with a coat of acrylic primer before adding a base coat of emulsion or acrylic paint. If the base coat is dark, stencil a thin coat of white paint on top. Apply your stencil and, if required, protect with a coat of clear varnish when it is completely dry.

FABRIC

Use special fabric paint for stencilling on fabric and follow the manufacturer's instructions carefully. Place card or blotting paper behind the fabric while working and keep the material taut. If you are painting a dark fabric, best results are achieved by stencilling first with white or a lighter shade. Heat seal the design following the manufacturer's instructions.

CERAMICS

Use special ceramic paints to work directly onto glazed ceramic tiles, and unglazed ceramics such as terracotta. Make sure all surfaces are clean, so that the stencils can be fixed easily. Apply the paint with a brush, sponge, spray or mini-roller. Ceramic paints are durable and washable, and full manufacturer's instructions are given on the container.

GLASS

Before applying the stencil make sure the glass is clean, spray on a light coat of adhesive and place the stencil in position. Spray on water-based or ceramic paint, remove the stencil and allow to dry. If you wish to stencil drinking glasses, use special non-toxic and water-resistant glass paints. An etched-glass look with stencils on windows, doors and mirrors can be achieved with a variety of materials.

PAINTED SURFACES

Stencils can be applied to surfaces painted with matt, satin or vinyl silk emulsion, oil scumble glazes, acrylic glazes and varnishes, and to matt wallpaper. If you wish to decorate a gloss surface, stencil first with an acrylic primer, leave to dry and then stencil the colours on top. Surfaces to be stencilled need to be smooth so that the stencil can lay flat.

PATCHWORK TABLECLOTH

Red and white checks seem to conjure up the instant warmth of a farmhouse. With just a few basic shapes, combined totally at random, it is easy to create a pattern that looks a great deal more complicated than it really is. This project requires patience in planning, but the end result is incredibly satisfying – a tablecloth that is crying out for a steaming pot of tea and copious quantities of home-made scones and jam to be set upon it.

PAINT COLOUR GUIDE

Bright red   Cream   White

PAINTING THE TROMPE L'OEIL CLOTH

1 Map out freehand with a faint pencil line where you want the tablecloth to be. If you are working on bare wood, prime it. Paint the base colour of the cloth in a cream emulsion.

2 When dry load up a paintbrush with the same cream colour and paint a ridge on the edge of the cloth. Do this by slightly twisting the brush outwards, away from the cloth towards the wood. Paint in a white line to finish the edge.

3 Stencil the solid red square shapes first (stencil G).

4 Fill in the empty squares at random. Stand back every so often to check that the different elements are evenly distributed.

5 Stencil a line of stitches (stencil B) along the outside edge. Finally, varnish the cloth.

PROJECT PATTERN

The pattern in the photograph opposite is built up of alternating red squares and motifs of your choice in between.

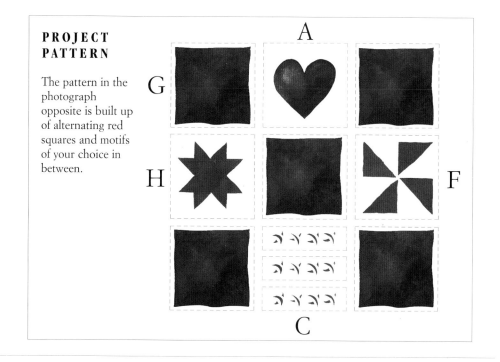

PAINTING THE EDGE OF THE CLOTH
To make the cloth look more three-dimensional, paint a ridge on the outside edge and finish it off with a thin white line. This will give the illusion that the cloth is sitting on top of the table rather than painted on.

MARKING OUT THE SQUARES
Find the centre of the cloth and draw inside stencil G in pencil to mark out the first square. Draw lines across the square from corner to corner and extend them to the edge of the cloth. Mark 13 cm (5¼ in) intervals along these lines. Following the direction of the first square, link the lines together to create a grid, enabling you to position the stencil card easily.

PLACING THE MOTIFS
Stencil the non-symmetrical shapes in all directions so that they can be viewed from all angles. For example, position a heart facing up in one square, down in the next, or left and right. Finally, rub out any remaining lines and put on a couple of layers of varnish. An oil-based varnish makes the surface slightly heat resistant and gives a yellow tinge, which unifies the whole surface.

By painting the patchwork design in blue and yellow ochre you can create a softer look, perhaps lifted with just a little red for warmth. An unusual variation would be to paint a wall-hanging using the double stitch stencil D as fringing. The motifs can be used to give impact in small areas and in more muted shades they could be used to create a Shaker-style design.

SQUARE AND HEART MOTIF (STENCILS A AND G)

BELOW: STITCHED HEART BORDER (STENCILS A AND D)

ABOVE: STAR TILES (STENCIL H)

RIGHT: HEARTS STRIPES (STENCILS A AND C)

LEFT: SQUARE AND WINDMILL BLOCKS (STENCILS F AND G)

STAR AND STITCH BORDER (STENCILS B, G AND H)

BIRD AND CROSS STITCH REPEAT (STENCILS C AND E)

RIGHT: STITCHED SQUARE BLOCKS (STENCILS B AND G)

LEFT: WINDMILL TILES (STENCILS F AND G)

RIGHT: STITCHED SQUARE REPEAT (STENCILS D AND G)

WINDMILL BLOCKS (STENCIL F)

REFLECTED HEARTS BORDER (STENCILS A AND B)

CARROTS & RADISHES

Clean, crisp, crunchy-looking vegetables look realistic enough to eat in this project. Spiky-shaped carrots are combined with rounded radishes, all looking as if they have just been dug up, had the earth shaken from them and washed under freezing cold tap water. Dark red, bright orange and lime green are used for a bold effect. The design works best if positioned halfway up the wall or at the top to form arches that seem to dangle from the ceiling.

PAINT COLOUR GUIDE

Bright orange	Lime green	Dark green
Deep red	Cream	

PAINTING A WALL FRIEZE

1 Coat the wall in an off-white emulsion paint and then give it a washed look with a cream emulsion mixed with water and matt water-based glaze.

2 Draw a very faint line using a spirit level as a guide to position the stencils. Paint the carrots and radishes stencils alternately.

3 When the design is dry give the whole wall a coat of water-based satin varnish to protect it from the grease and grime of everyday wear and tear. Satin varnish is more practical in the kitchen than a matt coat as it repels condensation, steam and general dirt.

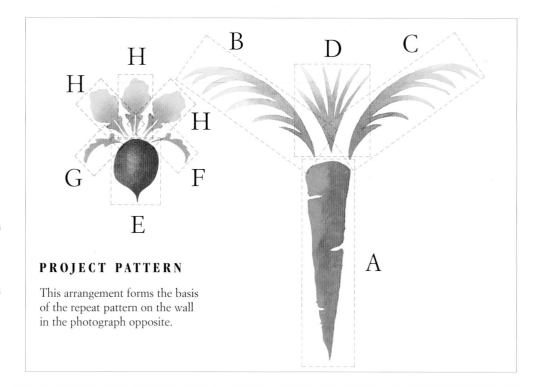

PROJECT PATTERN

This arrangement forms the basis of the repeat pattern on the wall in the photograph opposite.

BLENDING THE LEAF COLOURS

To prevent colours merging within a single shape work first with one colour from one end of the shape. Then use a separate brush to work from the other end towards the first colour. Keep a brush solely for blending and clean the mixing brush on kitchen paper between each use to blend the colours cleanly.

GIVING DIMENSION TO THE SHAPES

The radishes will look more realistic if you paint round the outside of the shape with a swirling motion, leaving a touch of the background colour showing in one area as a highlight. Do not worry if you apply the paint heavily in areas – you can overpaint the mistake with the background colour.

STIPPLING THE LEAVES

A stippled effect can lift the look of a project like this, giving it more visual movement. Stencil a shape and wait for it to dry. Then take a clean brush with very little paint on it and dab the paint gently over the existing colour.

VARIATIONS

These carrots and radishes can be arranged in many ways as well as a frieze. Why not paint bunches of carrots hanging like strings of onions? Experiment with different combinations on paper before you start work on a project and plan the positions of the shapes. There is nothing more frustrating than wishing one element was slightly to the left or not there at all!

CARROT TOP STRIPES (STENCIL D)

RIGHT: CARROT CRACKER (STENCILS A AND D)

RADISH LEAVES FRIEZE (STENCILS F AND G)

**RADISH ROOTS PYRAMID
(STENCIL E)**

RADISH LEAF BORDER (STENCIL H)

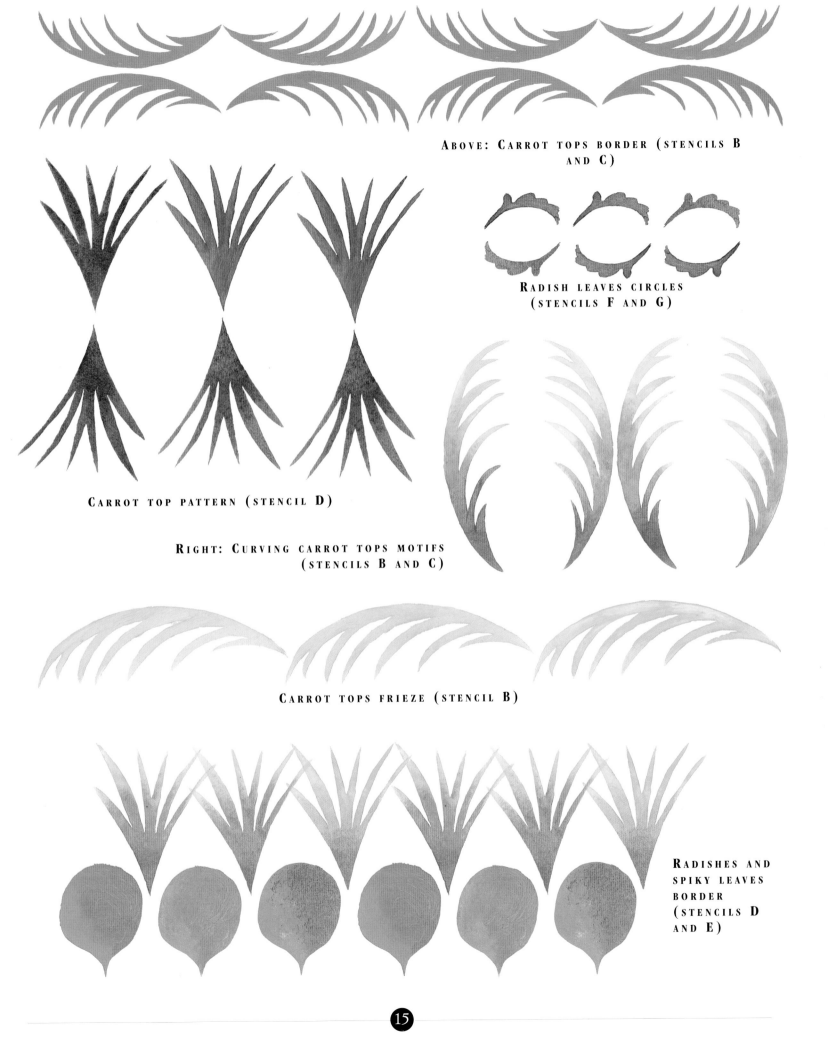

ABOVE: CARROT TOPS BORDER (STENCILS B AND C)

RADISH LEAVES CIRCLES (STENCILS F AND G)

CARROT TOP PATTERN (STENCIL D)

RIGHT: CURVING CARROT TOPS MOTIFS (STENCILS B AND C)

CARROT TOPS FRIEZE (STENCIL B)

RADISHES AND SPIKY LEAVES BORDER (STENCILS D AND E)

PAINT COLOUR GUIDE

Muted Purple	Dusky cream
Terracotta	Gold

PAINTING A TILED EFFECT

1 Paint the wall in a dark cream emulsion to simulate a grout colour.

2 Work out the size of your tiles. Draw them out on the wall, with the aid of a spirit level, leaving a 1 cm (⅜ in) gap in between each tile.

3 Divide a roll of masking tape lengthwise using a scalpel so that you have tape 1 cm (⅜ in) wide. Stick the tape where you require the grout lines.

4 Mix up different shades of emulsion with matt glaze and paint the tiles. Remove the tape. You will be left with squares of colour.

5 Stencil the lattice first (stencils E and F) and fill in the round blank space with feathers, ducks or chickens.

6 Give the whole surface a couple of layers of varnish.

W arm, rich aubergine, terracotta and earth tones conjure up a cosy farmhouse feel, with ducks and chickens in brilliant gold for a touch of sophistication. These traditional rustic colours immediately suggest a welcoming atmosphere. Just imagine the smells of freshly baked bread wafting through the kitchen and smoking log fires – utter bliss. You can use this project to create a tiled effect, transforming a town kitchen or breakfast room, or enhancing your rural surroundings, quickly and easily.

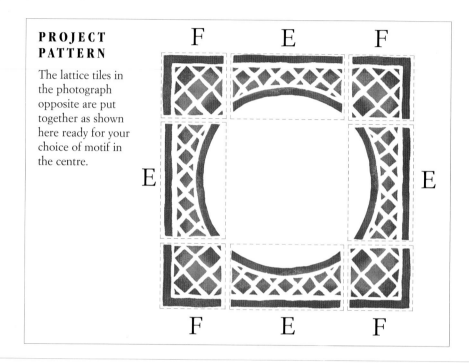

PROJECT PATTERN

The lattice tiles in the photograph opposite are put together as shown here ready for your choice of motif in the centre.

POSITIONING THE LATTICE

To position the lattice stencil F mark the stencil card with permanent marker to correspond with the tile lines behind. It does not matter if the stencils are not exactly straight, it will just add to the hand-painted look, but it is worth trying to keep them more or less in line.

APPLYING METALLIC GOLD PAINT

Using a metallic paint is slightly more difficult than an ordinary paint. You need to apply it more thickly to achieve an opaque look that really shines. Work on two tiles at the same time so that each stage can dry and you do not smudge the work you have just done.

PAINTING THE BIRDS

To emphasize the gold and to give the chickens and ducks depth it is a good idea to stencil some of the birds in a dark colour first and work on top with gold when dry. This also helps to give the bird shapes a well-defined outside edge.

DUCKS & CHICKEN LATTICE VARIATIONS

This project seems to suit muted earth tones best, but you could try any combination of colours. The feathers would look especially good in bright hues as an all-over wall design, floating and drifting on the surface. You could stencil the ducks and chickens in regimental rows or place them randomly as if waddling and pecking round the farmyard.

QUILLS BORDER (STENCIL D)

RIGHT: BIRDS FRIEZE (STENCILS A AND C)

LATTICE TILE (STENCIL F)

BELOW: BIRDS AND LATTICE EDGING (STENCILS A, C AND E)

FEATHERS MOTIF (STENCIL D)

ABOVE: LATTICE
EDGING
(STENCIL E)

LATTICE FRIEZE
(STENCIL E)

FLOATING FEATHERS
(STENCIL B)

ABOVE: CHICKEN
ROUNDELAY
(STENCILS A
AND F)

RIGHT: LATTICE
CORNER
(STENCIL F)

PEAS & BEANS

Trailing, tangled pea and bean leaves and pods are combined here to create an orderly, yet delicate, border design. The motifs give a country feel of newly picked produce, but the colours take the project into the area of modern interior design. Cool, fresh turquoise with green and cream, highlighted with stark white, creates a clean, crisp effect in contrast to the distressed, washed effect of the dado rail and tongue and groove boarding below.

PAINT COLOUR GUIDE

Turquoise   Bright green

Cream   White

CREATING A BORDER FRIEZE

1 Paint the wall with turquoise emulsion paint.

2 Carefully plan the design and measure the position of the stencils using tracing paper before painting them. Use green and cream paint for the running border of leaves (stencils A, C, D, G and H), with the pod stencil B repeated in pairs in green. When dry, paint cream peas and beans in the pods (stencils E and F).

3 Paint the dado rail in white first, then apply a cream wash on top.

4 Similarly paint the tongue and groove boarding, but use a turquoise base and a cream wash on top.

PROJECT PATTERN

This arrangement forms the basis of one repeat pattern on the wall in the photograph opposite. The peas and beans are stencilled on top of the pods.

PLANNING THE DESIGN
Position the stencils in your pattern and draw the outlines on tracing paper. You can use this tracing to position your stencils all the way through the repeat. Simply attach the tracing to the wall with masking tape and lift it up and down to slot in the appropriate stencil card.

MATCHING THE REPEAT
To achieve an exact repeat every time, when you have finished the first pattern move the tracing along the wall to where you want the design to be. Now with a marker pen trace through the position of the first painted stencil so that all subsequent repeats will be equidistant.

HIGHLIGHTING THE MOTIFS
To lift the design use white on the tops and edges of the leaves to highlight them. This gives the frieze a more delicate look and adds more dimension to the leaf shapes.

PEAS & BEANS VARIATIONS

The rambling nature of these stencil designs makes this project incredibly versatile. You can twist and twine the patterns around corners of walls or even floors. You can even make them appear to grow over furniture and up onto the wall behind. Choose a starting point and simply let the stencil designs flow as naturally as possible. Remember to stand back every so often to check that the stencils look balanced.

VEGETABLE LEAVES BORDER (STENCILS A AND G)

REFLECTED TENDRIL EDGING (STENCIL H)

ABOVE: LEAVES AND TENDRILS BORDER (STENCILS C AND H)

PEA PODS FRIEZE (STENCILS B AND E)

LEFT: BEANS IN A ROW (STENCIL F)

BEAN PODS BORDER (STENCILS B AND F)

ABOVE: LINKING LEAVES REPEAT (STENCIL C)

**PEA PODS AND
LEAVES FRIEZE
(STENCILS A AND B)**

LEAF CIRCLE (STENCILS A, C, G AND H)

**FLOWERS AND PEAS IN ROWS
(STENCILS D AND E)**

A wash of bright lime colour with tulips in viciously bright pink and green gives this storage cupboard a more contemporary look. Painting the chicken wire silver keeps the metallic feel, while a light wash of yellow ochre as a ground for the design maintains the rustic character. By positioning the tulips haphazardly on the cupboard you can just imagine the back door of the kitchen blowing open before someone shuts out the cold air and the room returns to a safe, warm haven.

PAINT COLOUR GUIDE

Lime green	Yellow ochre	Cream
Bright pink	Silver	

PAINTING A STORAGE CUPBOARD

1 Prime bare wood, then apply cream emulsion.

2 Apply a lime-coloured wash to the outside areas and an ochre wash to the stencil background. The washes consist of emulsion paint diluted with water.

3 Paint the chicken wire stencil A using silver metallic paint. Stencil petals (stencils B, D and E) in a haphazard arrangement and complete with the leaves stencils F and C.

4 Finally coat the whole surface with two layers of water-based varnish.

PROJECT PATTERN

This arrangement shows just one of the patterns used on the cupboard in the photograph opposite.

PLACING THE MOTIFS

With a dark pen, draw round the outside edge of each stencil motif onto paper. Cut round this following the shape exactly. Repeat the process a few times for each motif so that you have enough to build up your pattern. Stick the paper cutouts in the required positions with spray adhesive.

PAINTING THE CHICKEN WIRE DESIGN

Stencil across the surface with chicken wire (stencil A), painting right over the paper shapes. Wait for it to dry completely and then carefully peel the paper off. Peel one shape at a time so that you leave a clean outline.

ADDING THE TULIPS

Once the paper cutouts are peeled off, the clear negative spaces will be revealed. Lay the stencil cards on top of the negative spaces and stencil the tulips in bright pink, bringing the project to life. Similarly paint in the leaves in bright green.

TULIPS & CHICKEN WIRE VARIATIONS

T he chicken wire design looks equally effective as a background pattern or worked over the top of the other stencils. You could even experiment with tulips growing in and out of the wire. The flowers can be painted in bold, bright colours or in soft, pastel shades and, like any garden planting, look good in a variety of combinations. Experimentation is the key and the shapes can be used in a quite stylized manner if you wish.

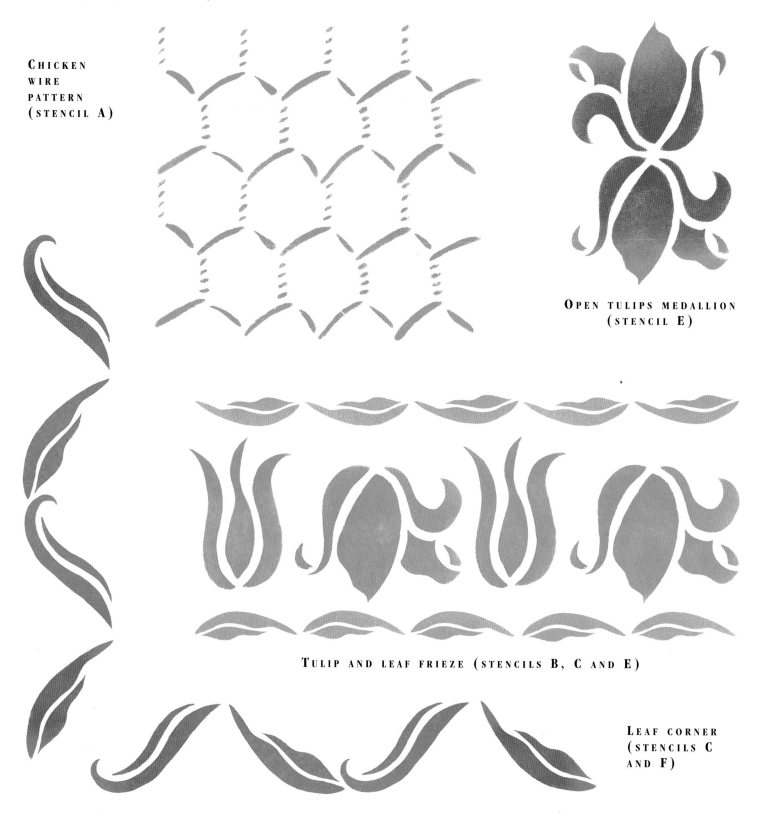

CHICKEN WIRE PATTERN (STENCIL A)

OPEN TULIPS MEDALLION (STENCIL E)

TULIP AND LEAF FRIEZE (STENCILS B, C AND E)

LEAF CORNER (STENCILS C AND F)

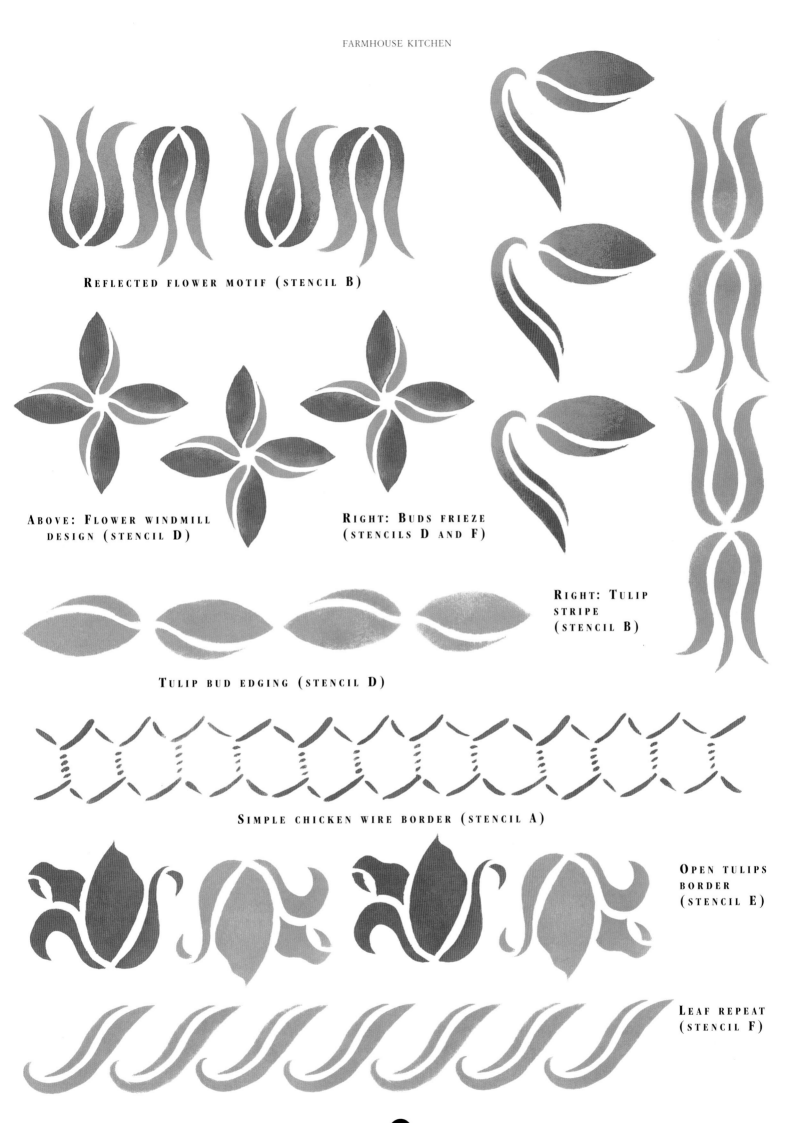

REFLECTED FLOWER MOTIF (STENCIL **B**)

ABOVE: FLOWER WINDMILL DESIGN (STENCIL **D**)

RIGHT: BUDS FRIEZE (STENCILS **D** AND **F**)

RIGHT: TULIP STRIPE (STENCIL **B**)

TULIP BUD EDGING (STENCIL **D**)

SIMPLE CHICKEN WIRE BORDER (STENCIL **A**)

OPEN TULIPS BORDER (STENCIL **E**)

LEAF REPEAT (STENCIL **F**)

HERBS & RIBBON

PAINT COLOUR GUIDE

Cream	Sage green
Cornflower blue	Purple

DECORATING THE PLATTER

1 Paint the wooden plate with primer and then with a coat of cream emulsion.

2 Mix a small amount of sage green emulsion with matt glaze and apply a wash to the plate using big sweeping movements.

3 Start the stencilling with the ribbon (stencil A) and build up the herbs from the bottom. Fill any gaps with sections of the stencils.

4 Use different gradations of colour to give variation and depth to the design.

5 Work your way round the perimeter of the plate and finish with a couple of layers of varnish to protect your stencilling.

T he calm, muted colours of sage green, clear blue and purple are ideal for creating a gentle rustic theme. Freshly gathered herbs tied together in bunches with a colourful purple ribbon and hanging from the kitchen beams to dry, conjure up the essence of country life. Sage, rosemary and thyme are all plants stored for use during the winter months for culinary purposes or herbal remedies, lotions and potions. Here they decorate the shelves and a wooden platter.

PROJECT PATTERN

The border on the plate in the photograph opposite is a simple repeat of this pattern; stencils are superimposed in a random manner to create the bunch of herbs in the centre.

F

E

MASKING OFF PARTS OF STENCILS
In this project the design is built up as you go along, sometimes using the whole shape of the stencil and sometimes masking off sections to fill in the gaps. Do not worry if shapes overlap – it adds to the end result and makes the herb bunch look more generous.

MEASURING FOR THE BORDER
To have a set repeat round the outside of the plate you will need to measure the design you want to use, then measure the space you want it to fit into. Simply divide the design length into the plate circumference and mark it onto the plate faintly in pencil as a guide. Use a tape measure for measuring.

GRADUATING COLOUR FOR DEPTH
By graduating the paint colour from light to dark within the stencil and repeating this in each subsequent shape you can achieve an undulating effect. This will give your design more visual movement.

HERB & RIBBON VARIATIONS

Sage green is a colour that seems instantly to suggest a country kitchen, but a much brighter blue-green is used here to good effect. The shape of the thyme sprigs allows them to be trailed wherever you wish and although the rosemary and sage are slightly more rigid in pattern they can also be placed in a multitude of designs. Bunches of herbs would look great stencilled as if hanging just below the ceiling.

REFLECTED STALK FRIEZE (STENCIL C)

RIGHT: TWISTED THYME BORDER (STENCIL E)

SAGE LEAF EDGING (STENCIL D)

ENTWINED RIBBONS BORDER (STENCIL A)

ABOVE: RIBBON EDGING (STENCIL A)

LEFT: SAGE LEAF BORDER (STENCIL D)

LEFT: REFLECTED STALK EDGING (STENCIL C)

ABOVE: SAGE
LEAF PATTERN
(STENCIL D)

RIGHT: LOOPED
RIBBON BOW
(STENCIL A)

ABOVE:
ROSEMARY
BORDER
(STENCIL B)

THYME SWAG
(STENCIL F)

RANDOM RIBBONS
(STENCIL A)

THYME CIRCLE
(STENCIL F)

31

SUPPLIERS

Emulsion paints are easily obtainable from DIY stores and good hardware stores; contact manufacturers below for your nearest supplier. Oil sticks and acrylic paints can be obtained from artists' materials stores. Other stencilling supplies can usually be found in any of the above and there are many dedicated stencil stores.

Imperial Chemical Industries plc
(ICI)
(Dulux paints)
Wexham Road
Slough
SL2 5DS
(Tel. 01753 550000)

Crown Decorative Products
PO Box 37
Crown House
Hollins Road
Darwen
Lancashire
(Tel. 01254 704951)

Fired Earth plc
Twyford Mill
Oxford Road
Adderbury
Oxfordshire
(Tel. 01295 812088)

ACKNOWLEDGEMENTS

Thanks to Kinnis, Mark Glenn, The Fanshaws, The Umbrian Contingent, Gina Hudson, Richard Tiley, Peter Watts, Graham Jones and Roy Tiley for their carpentry skills; to my Mum for her unconditional support; to Fred, Orlando, William, The Myers, Dimitri and Paddy Doherty just because; and finally to Karen, Caroline and Graeme.

Merehurst wish to thank the following for their help: Dulux Advice Centre; The Pier; Cargo Homeshops; The Home Place.

First published in 1998 by Merehurst Limited
Ferry House, 51–57 Lacy Road, Putney, London SW15 1PR

ISBN 1-85391-731-1

A catalogue record of this book is available from the British Library.

Commissioning Editor: Karen Hemingway
Introductory text: Julie Collins
Editor: Geraldine Christy
Designer: Roger Hammond
Photographer: Graeme Ainscough
Stylist: Caroline Davis

CEO & Publisher: Anne Wilson
International Sales Director: Mark Newman

Colour separation by Bright Arts (HK) Limited, Printed in Singapore

Katrina Hall divides her time between stencilling, paint effects and interior design for both commercial projects and private clients.

PATCHWORK TABLECLOTH

B

C

A

D

E

F

G

H

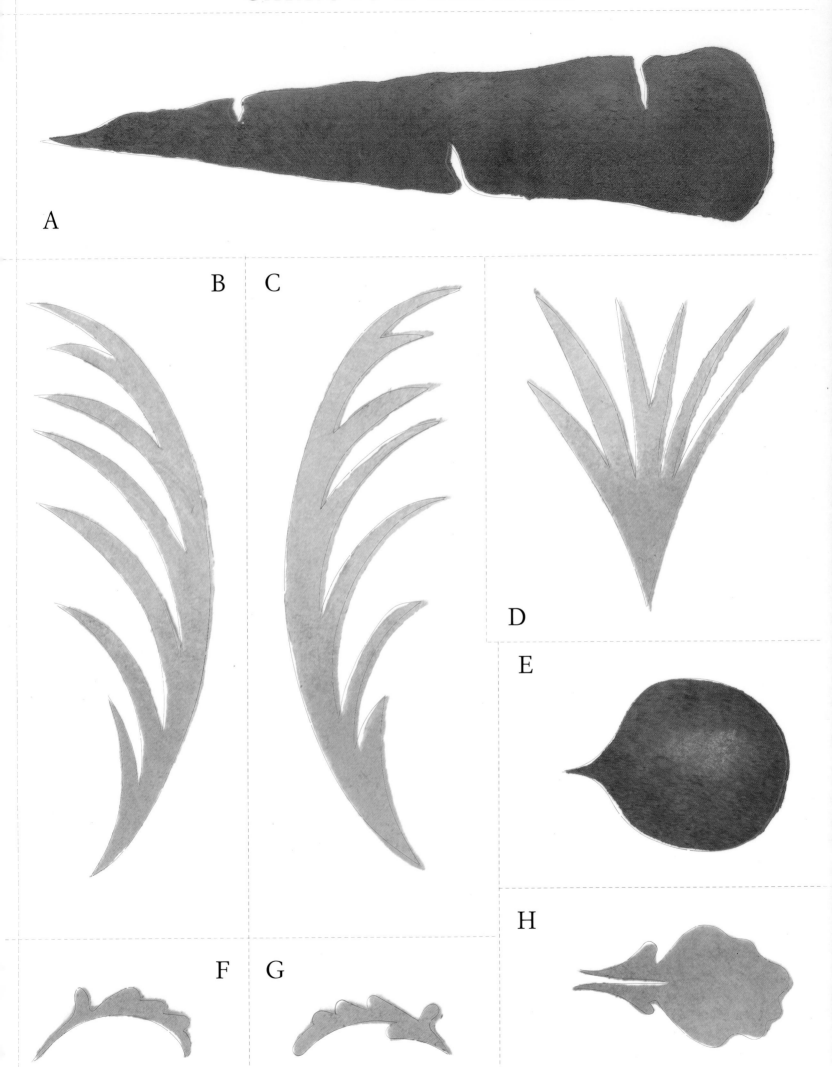

A

B

C

D

E

F

G

H

DUCKS & CHICKENS LATTICE

A

B

C

D

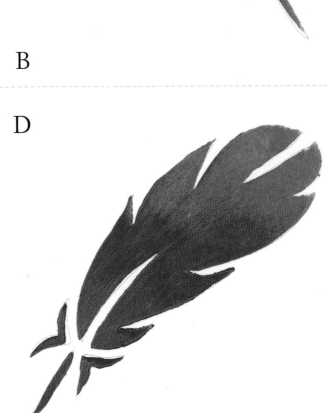

E

F

PEAS & BEANS

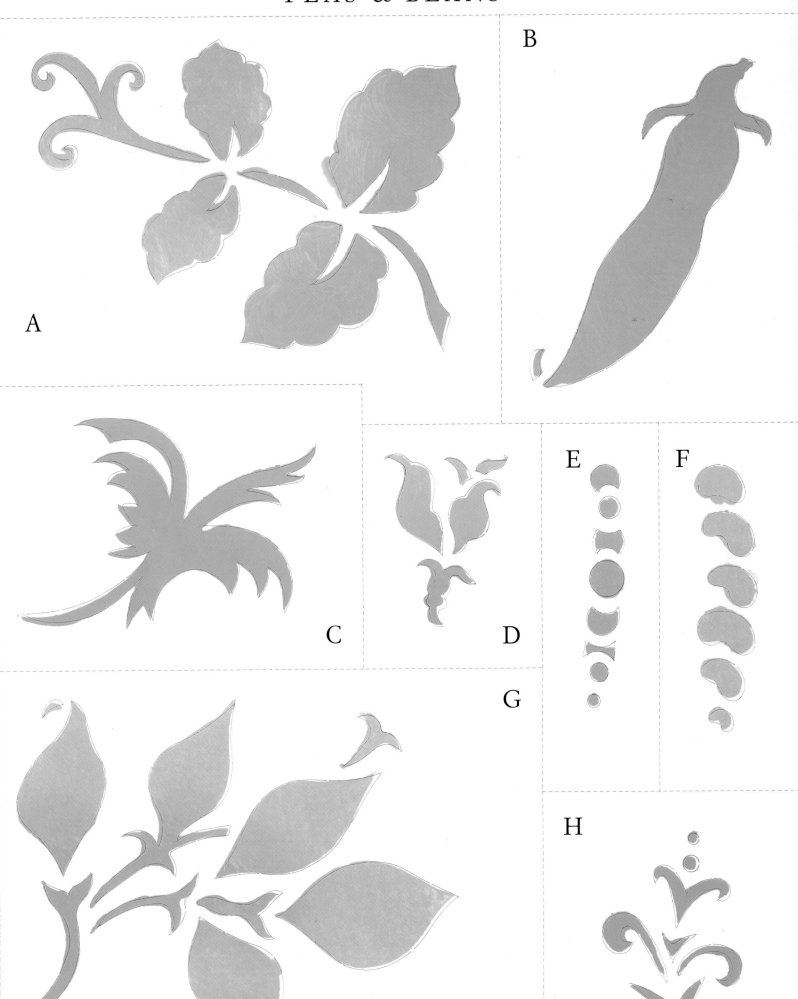

A

B

C

D

E

F